A View

MW00937382

Conversations With My Grandson

Mike Mallory & Tom Carroll

Cover Design and Art: RamaJon & Tom Carroll
Interior Design: RamaJon

Published by: T.H.Carroll Sales.

First Printing 2018
ISBN: 978-1721823635

Available through Amazon.com. For bulk orders and distributor pricing, contact:

La Grande Stereo - lagrande_stereo@hotmail.com

DEDICATION

Joey's parents, Kathy McDonald and Kris Mallory deserve special mention and an expression of appreciation from the authors for their contribution to this book. Even though they never appear directly in the text, mention is often made of them.

Kathy and Kris stand behind the pages adding their unique mixture of personalities and parenting wisdom. Easy to say, without them, Joey wouldn't be Joey.

Joey has another set of grandparents - Dave and Pam Mann. If, *A View From The Hot Tub* readers call for a sequel. Dave and Pam will certainly be called on to tell their side of the story.

PREFACE

A View From The Hot Tub is a collection of stories about my grandson. It's also a larger story about our family, and the positive effects of children, in this case, the impact my grandson has had on me.

Having boxed in amateur tournaments as a boy, I learned always to keep my guard up, a habit that has influenced me in other ways. Now far into adulthood I'm still guarded, always very careful when people try to tell me things. Despite this, my grandson manages to catch me flat-footed, unsuspecting and unprepared.

I've learned and unlearned quite a lot from this kid. I'm no longer as concerned about filtering every experience and not always on guard. At least not when it's Joey delivering the punches. My wife, Laura gets credit for softening me up too.

Everyone knows that parents and grandparents think their kids are the smartest ever born. The ten, now twelve-year-old who allowed us to join him in our hot tub took the, Brightest Kid Ever Born title to another level. What happened there, things said in the hot tub were just too good to stay in the tub.

The first stories appeared online in a series of Facebook posts. This revelation explains the repetition of some of the basics. Elements like the origin of the hot tub, Joey's peculiar habits and my unashamed and repeated praise for my two life coaches, my wife, and a ten-year-old boy.

The players are Joey Mallory, myself, and the family glue, my wife, Laura. Three people and a hot tub. All events happened as described and conversations are as accurate as memory allows. However, like my favorite writers, I never let the facts get in the way of a good story.

To my surprise, friends and strangers began commenting. With each new post the numbers grew. There's something about a kid who repeatedly out-smarts the adults in the room that triggers a laugh. I knew this - Laura and I were the first two laughing. Still, the public response was a major surprise.

From their comments I've learned that every family has a "Joey" or wants one. But Joseph DiMaggio Mallory stands out in a crowd. Of course he does, he's my grandson. Not that I'm unique, but after all the years, all the time that passed while I wasn't watching the calendar, I'm a grandparent, the stereotypical variety. Quick to give eye-rolls to others who got here before me, now I get it - totally.

Joey was our first grandchild. We have a second and third now. But the other two are still young. When they begin to show themselves, maybe I'll have the energy to do this again, to reveal more Mallory family antics.

For now, Joey's got a firm grip on our hearts and minds, commanding center stage. But it's my wife, Laura who holds the high ground. Laura's intelligence and big heart combine to interpret, and when necessary, ground his creative energy.

Laura gets credit for maintaining Joey's faith in adulthood as it's demonstrated in our house-hold. She carries treasure in her bag of tricks. I steal from her all the time. Jokes, observations, philosophy and cool phrases. Most of all I steal her mojo. Well, I try.

Laura always comes from a good place. She makes it seem effortless. I admire this trait. I've been lucky, the two of us have run the river together for over forty years. Her example of how to live has made my life easier. Oh yeah, much more fun too!

There is another name on the title page and cover; Tom Carroll. Tom is my pal. And pal is not a word I throw around. A real friend is hard to find. Friendship, like anything worthwhile, takes work.

This next statement seems unreal, but Tom and I have been friends for over 50 years. We don't need to be careful when we're around each other.

This book is Tom's vision. He saw possibility in my stories that I missed. In fact, when he offered to explore the possibility of a book I was slow to catch on and reluctant to help. With my guard up again, snide and snarky comments were all I had to offer. Tom stayed in the fight, knowing that I was just scared - knew that even after the favorable Facebook reception I was afraid the project would fail. He knows me well.

"It's supposed to be a book, not a pamphlet," he kept saying. When I did not make time or have the patience to expand, explain and fill in the holes, Tom did it for us. Please don't tell him, but I'm touched by his effort to re-write my ravings into something readable.

I'm still, and will probably always be amazed by the depth and originality of Joey's insight. When he's around I find myself wondering what will happen next. That might seem like a lot to lay on a kid. But hey, he started it! Maybe someday he will read this book and chuckle. I'm hoping that everyone who reads it gets a laugh - hoping all will experience something like the feeling Laura and I had while we were living these stories - a mixture of amazement and anticipation.

Thanks to Laura. Thanks to Tom. Thanks, especially to the one and only Joseph DiMaggio Mallory.

Finally, special thanks go to Nancy Coffelt, Karen Hefley and Robert Simpson for their editorial suggestions and patient reading of Tom's early re-writes and last drafts. Tom tells me that each of these three played an important part in making these stories readable.

One more thing. Tom asked me to come-up with better photos, high-rez originals instead of Facebook copies. I could not find them.

With this admission, I can state that any remaining errors are 100% Tom's fault. I love saying that!

With appreciation for all of you.

Mike Mallory – June, 2018

INTRODUCTION

A View From The Hot Tub is a series of stories about Mike, and his grandson, Joey. Or maybe it's the other-way-around. Either way, that's not where the book begins.

Mike and I met somewhere around 1968 - at least a lifetime ago. Over the years our paths have run parallel, sometimes diverged, but never separated for long. In the early years we shared high school classes and the stage as a Pop/Folk duo.

By 1972, Mike had already hooked up with Rock Creek Roll Band, a five-man, full time working band. For reasons long forgotten, I was included in the mix, booking club dates, promoting, and in some sense, managing the menagerie. Picture six young guys, band members and myself accompanied by wives, girlfriends and a half-ton of equipment. Imagine this circus traveling thousands of highway miles at the mercy of undependable vehicles.

See us setting up and playing shows for a night or a week, month after month, playing small halls and bars across six states. Close quarters for so many miles, and what, in memory, seems like an equal number of hotel rooms, guaranteed that everyone knew everyone - very well.

I've known Mike as a friend and fellow prankster. I've known Mike, the musician, through the eyes of his fans and our mutual friends. The point being that our multi-faceted friendship provided the perspective and latitude required for me to fill in and expand on Mike's original, shorter stories. As now, without a side-by-side comparison, neither he nor I are sure which one of us wrote what.

Being a parent and a grandparent, caring for and enjoying life with and through the lives of those we love, this is the obvious story and point of the book. Knowing ourselves, becoming comfortable with what life and others bring to us, or throw at us, what happens inside as we learn to look beyond ourselves - this is another perspective that made, *A View From The Hot Tub*, worth writing.

One or the other, or somewhere between, readers will find their own reasons for enjoying the characters, their conversations, the antics of life in the Mallory household.

In our younger years we were as full of ourselves as any two young guys could be. We thought we would never grow old. We still don't. The following, (slightly altered), lines from a Jerry Jeff Walker tune capture the tone:

Pissin' in the wind,
bettin' on a longtime friend

Makin' the same mistakes
we swore we'd never make again

And we're still pissin' in the wind,
laughin' as it blows on friends

We were gonna sit and grin,
and tell our grandchildren

Mike and I used to think that, "any day now" we'd have everything figured out. We assumed that if not already, then soon, we'd be wise enough to teach the children in our lives - anyone, for that matter - lessons for which they would be grateful. Now we see things differently. As Mike is about to tell you, it's all turned out better than he ever expected.

Tom Carroll – July, 2018

THE PARADE

As I began to recollect and write these stories Joey was ten-years-old. But like all children, he was born younger. Yes, that was an attempt at humor. And yet, packed into this remark is the source of great puzzlement. Kids start at zero, or so we think. How is it that they often out-run us in one or more lines of development way before they're old enough to shave or wear lipstick? Joey, for example, the things he did, things he said as a very young child gave us an idea of who we were dealing with and what was to come.

I hear fathers talk about looking forward to the time when the kids are old enough to do stuff with, as though the first few years are a waste of time. Turned right-side-up, that attitude is the real waste. If our grandson is any indicator, the good stuff starts early and just keeps getting better. The following is an example.

We took Joey to a parade not long after his fifth birthday. After assessing the crowd and those parading past him, he commented;

"I am not sure I understand parades. The people watching the parade are exactly like the people in the parade."

That's the way he has always talked - full sentences,

13

very formal. A style he couldn't have learned from anyone in the family.

Comedian Ryan Hamilton talks about a parade in his hometown in rural Idaho, population one thousand. On the 4th of July, all one thousand must participate. Five hundred watch from curbside, as the other five hundred, their friends and family members, parade past, marching or riding by on decorated cars and pick-ups.

Hamilton didn't say, but maybe the marchers and spectators switched places on alternating years. Either way, everyone involved looked the same. By the time Joey's five, long before his first trip to Idaho, he has this figured out.

Thinking of giant balloon figures and extravagant floats, I wonder what he'd say about Macy's extravaganza in New York? I might never know. But small-town parades? He nailed it!

Not so long ago, throwing candy into the crowd was standard practice. Joey's response?

"I will never eat candy people throw on the ground."

It's funny how some stuff can stick with you, like gum on the bottom of your shoe. I never ate another piece of parade candy.

Parades and candy; I don't expect readers to be awe-stricken, but this was five-year-old Joey. Another five years, he's a hammer and I'm his favorite nail.

Laura and I are no different than other grandparents who brag about their children's, children. Boasting aside, this kid has been an authentic source of amazement. We often turn to each other, asking, "Did he say what I think he said?" Unnerving, even startling at times, the answer has always been, "Yes!"

The parade? Like I said, Joey was just getting started.

WHAT REMAINS

We had a hot tub at the house we lived in for thirty-eight years. My wife, Laura Mallory loved it. After down-sizing, and without telling me her plan, Laura saved-up and paid to have a new one installed on the patio in back of our, also new, stripped-down pad. A very fancy model. Forget the price. I was sold on it immediately.

Joey liked it too. He liked it so much that it was the inspiration for one of his great ideas. According to Joey, time spent in the tub would be, as it continues to be, "Quiet Time." He was quick to make up rules like this for anyone who joins him during this solemn occasion.

Ironically, though not a surprise, the central activity of Quiet Time is a running commentary featuring the voice of Joey Mallory. This monologue lasts from the time he gets in until he decides it's time to get out. I say that this is unsurprising because, after all, Joey is only ten.

Sometimes, not often, but sometimes he acts his age. To a ten-year-old, anything is or can be anything. So, Quiet Time is never quiet And time? Maybe it's the result of that giant tub of hot water. Whatever, the time part of Quiet Time is fluid. For example, listening to Joey's rap, I often forget about our rules - forget about kids and bedtime. No, the truth is, I forgot about that back when I was his age. Now, on more than a few nights, a moon that was just rising when we slipped into the water is passing overhead on its way toward the opposite horizon before Joey signs off and we all get out. That's a long time to listen to anyone talk.

Did I tell you that Joey's only ten? I don't get how he does it, the time thing. Maybe he's got us hypnotized. I think he knows but he's not telling. Many, but not all these stories happen in the tub. This one played out in the living room - proof that Joey's inspiration is not just a large tub of hot water. The kid is versatile.

Remember that show, Kids Say the Darndest Things? Art Linkletter, then someone else hosted the series. Each episode proved the point. Kids do say amazing things. Like last night when Joey said something that still has my head spinning. I'd been spacing. Yes, I confess. I don't pay attention to everything he says. Now I'm wondering what gems I've missed.

A little set-up will help here. Joey's ideas about God are not the result of any coaching from us. We've never been a religious family. Still, I wear a Saint Christopher medallion and let's just say that I know there are things I don't know. What I do know is that you don't want to be the sidewalk evangelist telling me what those might be. Saint Chris and my allergy to door knocking preachers are pretty much the extent of Joey's religious education at my knee.

Kevin's two boys were here, the three of them deep in conversation. Anyway, Joey must have used the God word. Having heard it, I come to full attention just in time to catch it when he says;

"I tell people who are struggling with the concept of God to think of it this way; It's what was before and remains afterward."

Joey was polite enough not to mention it, but I'm sure my mouth was hanging open. Recovering from something like shock, I realize that he's not offering anything more, no further information about this particular pronouncement or his beliefs, in general.

In past conversations, he'd told me that his beliefs are no one's business. Still, I want him to tell me how he came up with his God theory. Interestingly, I'm the one who just said that you don't want to be an evangelist at my door. So, what don't I understand about, "No one's business"?

Kevin's boys have gone home. All is quiet at the Mallory household.

Silence.

I guess that's what remains afterward.

WHAT IT MEANS

My grandson hosts his very own TV show, running back-to-back episodes. Since Laura and I downsized and Joey commandeered the tub our small household has little time for channel surfing, the figurative, television kind of surfing. When our grandson is with us, which is quite a lot of the time, it's, The Joey Show!

Laura and I may be typical doting grandparents but not what you'd call indulgent. If he was a normal kid, the kind that says normal things, for Joey's sake and our sanity, we would not have to think twice about pulling the plug on his monologues. Instead, we're sort of addicted to them. Part of the attraction, call it fascination, is that each one is new. The kid's interesting.

For me to say this is significant, considering that I have the patience of a two-year-old, the attention span of a gnat when someone is talking at me. So, remarkable but true, we allow the Joey Show to run uninterrupted. Laura and I, his network executives, have offered him an open-ended contract with a benefits package that includes unlimited refrigerator access, clean sheets and of course, use of the hot tub.

The tub might be Joey's favorite place but it's not always the stage for his most arresting pronouncements, like the one in the previous chapter, his revelation of the identity of God. The highlight of this past week was Joey's opinion about how a writer should order the elements of a novel. The line that stuck with me was;

"A writer should never start a book by defining the antagonist of the story. That is just lazy."

This book writing thing; Joey's remark does not apply in any way to what I'm working on here. Still, I don't know if his statement is correct. The fact that I can't call it, one way or the other has introduced self-doubt. This is not like me at all. Dang! I wish I had better writing chops. As it turns out, some college experience would have been beneficial.

My teachers and guidance counselors, Phyllis Jambura and Gene Bolen, tried to convince me to enroll. Already a legend in my own mind I ignored their advice. Now I'm at the mercy of my grandson to inform me as to how to recognize good vs. bad writing.

At some point my son, Kris re-told a story about Ernest Hemingway. As it goes, Hemingway bragged that he could tell a story in any amount of words. Somebody said, "Six." Hemingway wrote, "For Sale. Baby shoes, never worn."

Not bad. Helps explain why Hemingway's a legend. Except for suspicions that it's a literary myth, that Ernest is not the one who wrote it. Either way, real-life events, and Mojitos were Hemingway's inspiration. My inspiration and advice often come from my son, Kris and his son, Joey. Both are very much, real-life.

But I should have back-stopped the present day by acting on the council of wise advisers. I should have followed the recommendation of those two High School teachers and done some college time.

Even so, many of the things they taught me, added to Joey's antics, inspired this book. These, and my friend and co-author keep me hacking away. I do not doubt that our combined efforts will add measurably to the body of English literature. If that sounds pretentious, apparently I've communicated effectively for once.

What's the point of all this? Joey's pronounce-ment about writers has set my head spinning.

Jumping back to his remark about the proper time to introduce an antagonist and lazy writers - two things. First: I know for a fact that I didn't know what an antagonist was when I was Joey's age. Second: I'm not sure why he holds this opinion. I wonder what Phyllis would say?

But at that moment, the moment he said it, I think he's right.

Is he? As far as writing goes, I suspect it's not all that important. But the speed of my agreement shows how malleable I can be when my grandson gets involved.

What does this mean?

It means that I'm a grandparent.

PILGRIMS AND PYTHONS

So far, I've not made something clear. It might seem to readers that I'm the audience, the sole recipient of Joey's wisdom. The truth is, many of the episodes I've recounted don't specifically include me. Joey directs his ideas to Laura. He doesn't rate my brain as being worth the price of the powder to blow it up. Having just used a cliché like that, I can't blame the kid.

Whatever his evaluation of his grandad, he's made his decision based on the fact that my philosophical mentors were Groucho Marx and The Three Stooges. I do things like pretend that I'm urinating in the hot tub. Makes me laugh every time! My tub mates? Not really. Joey and Laura have out-grown me.

I'm not sulking, I swear! Why did I think it necessary to tell you this? I'm not sure. Maybe it's Joey. Ordinarily, I demand center stage and the microphone. Considering that I'm now content to relax and wait for my services to be called upon, to wait for the privilege of playing Joey's stooge, Maybe he's a good influence on me or something.

Now, back to the latest from the hot tub, and Joey's evolving world of ideas.

Tonight he opens the show, saying;

"I think that one of the reasons we may not fully respect the land and environment the way some cultures do is because we are not indigenous."

Notice that he says "indigenous," not, "Indians." I think he's waxing PC. But having learned my manners from Groucho, how would I know?

He's basing his thoughts on current news of giant pythons in Florida. The ones people buy at pet shops and abandon after they get big enough to eat the dogs they buy at those same stores. With growing regularity the nightly news delivers scare stories, news of human encounters and devastation visited on wild life by monster-size, predatory snakes. I think there's even a reality show now, Python Hunters of The Everglades. If not, maybe there should be.

But thinking that these deadly giants are just lurking deep in the Everglades is a mistake. Now they're back in town stalking their former owner's homes and lurking outside pet shops. Not picky eaters, they swallow anything unlucky enough to cross their path. Mid-day, they beat the heat by commandeering private swimming pools. It's an invasion!

"Maybe there are no natural predators for pythons in Florida," Joey adds.

Then came the leap, as he tells me;

"Pythons are like the massive immigration of Europeans to the United States a few centuries ago. Like pythons, America's immigrants disrupted the natural balance."

Do I agree? It doesn't matter to him. Like I said a couple of paragraphs ago, the conversation didn't directly include me. It's just my good fortune to be allowed in the tub when this and similarly weighty snippets fall from the kid's lips.

Joey has been speaking to Laura, the second most original thinker among the three of us. However smart I may not be, I have the good sense not to contest the prevailing assumption. Facts are facts. What's true here is that a sixty-four-year-old man with little more than a hot tub and bedroom to offer is not the pack leader.

Freed from leadership responsibilities I'd been working on a new angle to my, Peeing in The Tub, routine. Joey's Pilgrim and Pythons, idea stops me cold. Again, I didn't think of things like this at ten. To be honest, I don't think that way now. If Joey were like other kids, he would have stuck with the pet part of the snake thing, promising not to let another snake get loose in Florida if I'd buy him one. Since we live in Oregon, this would probably be true.

Back to his Python and Pilgrim comparison, debate or disagree, it's a sophisticated analogy. Once again, I'm impressed. Then my mind wanders.

The idea of tropical snakes in a northern climate spins me off into an imagined Christmas scene. Two snakes exchanging gifts in their winter den, one giving the other a pair of mittens. "Perfect," says the second snake, "I was out of bait."

Choosing not to suffer another one of his withering stares, I kept my imaginary snake riff to myself. Besides, I can save the jokes and slapstick gags for my bunk-mates at the old farts home where I may need all the material I can gather. In the meantime, I've held out long enough. It's time I grew up. I'm packing up and emigrating to the adult side of the hot tub. Will this disrupt the natural balance? I doubt that Joey or Laura will even notice.

Never-the-less, thanks to Joey, I'm opening to a world of ideas, like the effects of giant pythons in Florida. News today says someone wrangled a seventeen-footer. If the Pilgrims had landed in Florida, I'm wondering if we'd be eating stuffed snake or alligator for Thanksgiving dinner?

I want to run this by Joey, but you guessed it... It's Quiet Time.

G-MAN - AN INTERLUDE

I've made a decision. Having connected the dots, I see that the stars are aligned. After watching an interview with the Rolling Stones, I have decided to enter politics.

It was The Rolling Stones that turned my attention to public service. In October of 2016, somewhere past the forty-year mark in their career, they took to the stage at Desert Trip, that historic concert outside of Indio California. It was an epic line-up. The Stones shared the stage with Dylan, Neil Young, The Who, and Paul McCartney. Man, I wish I'd been there!

During an interview following the show, Keith Richards slid in a one-liner that I'll remember for years. Asked how it felt to have Nobel winning poet, Bob Dylan open for him, Richards said that he loved hearing Bob, and added that he, Richards, should be given a Nobel Prize for chemistry. Summing up a life lived in the spotlight and shadow of death - this in a dozen words or less - that was poetry.

Hearing the story, ending as it does with Richards' remark, I realized that I've always cared more about what Keith Richards had to say, compared to any politician.

A few weeks go by and The Stones are in the news again. It's late November, and they're set to release their first studio album in over a decade. The story circulating is that having gathered at British Grove Studios in West London, what was supposed to be a warm-up was good enough that as the notes of a final chord faded, musicians and engineers looked at each other and agreed, "This is what it's gonna be!" They finished the remaining tracks in three days.

The result was the equivalent of a live recording. Not live on stage, just the four of them and a trio of long-time sidemen in the studio, ripping through tunes with no overdubs, each song perfect on the first take. Then, like a sign or something, Eric Clapton happens to be at Grove, and steps in to add his unmistakable signature, filling out the song list at an even dozen.

Okay, great story. But that's not why I'm excited. As I started to say, if asked - *Drum Roll* - I will accept a position in the President's cabinet, Secretary of Rock 'n' Roll! These Stones stories kick-started me, igniting my already fermented imagination. With Kid Rock threatening a run for the Senate, my idea is pure genius. What does a Secretary of Rock 'n' Roll do? There's time to figure that out. In the meantime, I'd have great health and dental, even retirement benefits.

Yes, I'm supposed to be listening to Joey. But the President wants people who think outside the tub. I just did that. In fact, I do it regularly and so well that it justifies latitude for me from my prospective employer. As a Cabinet Member, I'd serve at the pleasure of the President. Still, me being me, I'll walk into my new office with an agenda, maybe an attitude. A mixture of the two might get me the media attention I crave.

There are a couple of things about which neither my staff nor I will tolerate argument. The Beatles and The Stones, these two groups are the best ever. Save your namby-pamby, multi-level thinking. Cutting to the chase, there will be no talk of rock 'n' roll being rooted in the work of Buddy, Little Richard, Muddy and Chuck Berry.

Exercising my secretarial powers, anyone not following my agenda will receive a weekend bird hunting trip with Dick Cheney. Shotguns and a half rack will be supplied. Oh Yeah; Donnie and Marie will be played continuously during your weekend with Dick.

In closing, I urge everyone to contact the White House now. Tell them, "Mallory is willing to serve." Don't say, "Mike," as this could get me confused with current VP, Pence. I'm ready to sever all music industry connections, recording deals, action figure contracts, any potential conflicts of interest. And I'll disclose my tax returns as soon as I file them. I'm qualified, no matter what Joey says.

This mention of Joey is not gratuitous, these musings have taken place in the hot tub. Shifting focus I looked up to see Joey giving me his dead-eye stare. It was over almost sooner than it began, but I swear he's read my mind.

The water was above a hundred degrees. Still, I could feel my cheeks flushing, my face growing even redder. A telepathic moment, things like this happen here in the tub. He'd gotten the psychic download and now he's thinking;

"Peapa," (that's what he calls me), *"Peapa's suffering from delusions of grandeur."*

I waited for more, something audible.

The kid never said a word.

MYSTIC PIZZA

Joey's Quiet Time. I don't recall needing quiet time when I was ten. Different era, different kids. At least Joey is.

Like most nights when Joey's here, we're in the tub, and it's Quiet Time again. Laura and I are going with the program, he's got us well trained. Joey treats the hot tub like it's his pulpit and himself, the high priest. What does that make Laura and me?

Last night the tub was cranked while the temperature outside hovered on the low side of 20 degrees and several inches of snow lay on the ground. Immune to the cold, Joey scrambled in and out of the tub, cooling off and chasing his dog. Yes, he was only in a swimming suit. No, I didn't mention it to him.

We're a live and let live - or die family. Not cruel but forward thinking, we believe our approach strengthens the gene pool.

At one point during his speed rap, Joey looked up at the heavens and said;

"The violet sky makes it look warm but faded around the edges."

With no idea what this means or how it could be true, I look up anyway. Don't ask me to explain - call it a transcendental, mystical moment. I saw it too, I knew what he meant.

Something Laura and I don't say much about is the shared knowledge that this is a special time, a year, maybe two and the hot tub will be in Joey's rear-view mirror. The smart move? We leave him free to expound uninterrupted from the time he gets in until he heads for the shower.

Laura is quiet and thoughtful, her occasional remarks, encouraging. My contribution is a shake or nod of my head, often with my mouth open. These are involuntary reactions. All the while, Joey's fulfilling his priestly duties. I haven't said it to Laura but I think we might be devotees. A devoted audience of three, Laura, myself, and the ears of the universe. The ears of whatever, "*was before and remains afterward.*"

The mood changes. We're hungry, so the party moves inside where the evening's show-stopping line was delivered along with a pizza Joey has already ordered from Domino's.

Unlike myself, he's memorized our credit card and pin numbers. On average, he orders a large cheese pizza twice a week. Each one lasts two, no more than three days. So far, he hasn't abused his privileges. I doubt that he will. Domino's will probably remain on speed dial.

At some point, Laura had realized that he's been donating to St. Jude Children's Hospital along with every purchase. What caught her attention were one-dollar donations to St. Jude's that coincided with every pizza ordered. Remembering St. Jude's TV appeals, those commercials they make featuring smiling children with telling, shiny heads. Laura decided to have a conversation about the extra expenditure. She mentioned to him that he had already donated.

"Mamo, children are not supposed to be sick," says Joey.

The result of this conversation? Our pizzas are going to cost a few bucks more than the price on the menu. We rule with an iron hand. No bleeding heart kid is pushing us around.

Saint Jude's is now on speed dial too.

ALL IN THE CARDS

I recently discovered a dark secret regarding my wife that has already changed the dynamic of our marriage. She made the mistake of revealing that she's an unbelievably poor sport. I now have huge advantage, a ton of leverage!

Joey and Laura play chess. The first matches were supposed to be just for training purposes. Laura's teaching style was practical, call it life-like, right down to the pools of Joey's blood on the floor at the end of each lesson. The two of them are now more evenly matched. No surprise, he's a fast learner, and their games have become highly competitive.

Last night Joey took Laura's queen early-on. What I heard spewing from her lips was shocking. I was mortified, my psyche is bruised. Judging by the cackling I heard from Joey, I suspect he is handling her tirade better than a fragile soul like me.

My new-found leverage? I am forever fortified - will never again pay the slightest attention to Laura's responses to my Three Stooges gags. I will no longer suppress any of the hilarious material that comes to my mind so naturally. All the stuff I've been pressured to bottle-up inside?

No more!

"Cuss away, Dear."

I couldn't be happier.

HIGHER POWERS

Joey tells me that he has an unpleasant physical reaction to boring people. His speed-raps in the hot tub, his conversations with Laura and I are never boring. This tells me that he wasn't exaggerating, and really knows the difference. Whatever, this kid makes me laugh.

Last night, Joey and his younger cousins had themselves a video conference, a virtual meeting type conversation about two of the greatest mysteries of life. They were asking each other the big questions;

"Why do bad things happen to good people?"
And, "Why does God allow children to suffer?"

These two are perennial, up there in the top-ten questions we all ask sooner or later. These three kids are leaning toward, sooner. I didn't feel the same pressing need to know these things when I was eight, or even, two years later as a Joey size, ten-year-old.

The conversation continued via Skype. That's another thing. If I'd have talked with my friends about stuff like that, it wouldn't have been on the phone. Telephones were for serious business in 1962. And Skype? In the 60's, Skype was nothing more than a misspelling - maybe skip, or type.

"Calling all cars!" Fact is, the comic creators of Dick Tracy never even considered attaching a TV screen to his cutting-edge, two-way radio. Don't believe me? Google it on your i-Watch.

But enough. More than just showing my age, I'm being a bore and ruining the story. The boys are nonchalantly navigating a three-way video call. This was 2017, no big deal. Add in the fact that I'm eavesdropping. I can't see the screen, but their conversation is still better than cable TV.

So, these three were Skyping and the conversation was serious. Their conclusion? The Three Young Wise Men decide that these questions are the reasons people have any questions or doubts regarding religious practice and faith. Made sense to me.

The best part of the conversation? The younger cousins believe - do not doubt - that Santa exists. There's no crisis of faith among this crew. Regardless of when you may be reading this;

A MERRY CHRISTMAS SEASON TO ALL!

DOCTOR MY EYES

There are three towns in the US named Boise. We took a trip to the one in Idaho last week. This is a recurring expedition. A hundred and sixty miles one-way, once a month to the Eye Doc.

Joey rates the places we stop for gas and food on the one-to-ten scale, based on how clean the bathrooms are kept. He's a bit of a germ freak. However, he's still a kid, and sometimes his germ phobia doesn't translate to his own teeth or the rest of his body. Girls are a few short years away. He'll figure it out.

Back to the bathrooms, he's decided that he wants a blacklight. Just like in a scene from CSI, his blacklight will be used to inspect all surfaces before he touches any one of them. Throw in a box of those crime scene type rubber gloves, a white lab coat and a pair of goggles to complete the costume. This could be good!

I called his Dad, Kris, and relayed the news. Kris's take is that the blacklight is a bad idea, and Joey should just assume that all truck stop bathrooms are dirty.

Mildly disappointed by Kris's response, I'm thinking that it would be totally funny to see the reaction of truckers with Joey in the john, blacklight in hand, examining the urinals, stalls, sink, and doorknob. I'm on the digicam as Joey narrates the show, a running commentary on his investigation. In years to come it'll be priceless.

But Dad said no, so we're out-a-there. I've got to see the doc.

I'm getting work done in my left eye - hypodermic needle, type work. The treatments aren't pleasant. Do I need to explain this?

Still, over-all it's a great day. I've got memories of Joey and his ideas to entertain me. Ignoring his Dad, I might just buy Joey that light. I've got enough stuff on Kris to last a lifetime.

So, a video titled; Joey Mallory Sanitizes the World, One Truck Stop at a Time.

This could still happen.

ALL FOR GOOD REASONS

I'd been wronged! Laura stayed out all night without even calling to tell me she was not coming home. I thought I *had* her and could hardly wait to tell Joey. He's here at the house and we're out back in the hot tub. Now's my chance. Of course, I'm breaking the rule, the Quiet Time rule. Joey talks and I'm expected to listen. But this material is too good, the perfect set-up for some deep male bonding.

Before he could start his lecture on the human condition I launched, telling him that Mamo stayed out all night and I was worried sick! I have never said those words - never said that I was, "worried sick." It felt good, and I was expecting him to side with me, already counting the months we could hold it over her head. Joey and I, the two of us teamed up and making Laura's life miserable. Am I pumped, or what!

Fully expecting him to supply the supporting lines that will put the game in play, I ask if she should be chastised for her actions. Imagine my disappointment when he says;

"No, we live in a free country. She is an adult. She takes responsibility for her actions."

Once again he speaks in full sentences, no contractions. And in this situation, way-too adult.

I should have stopped. Had I known what was coming I would have ended the game. Instead, I pushed my idea, sure that Joey has no clue how much fun he's about to miss. I'm on the verge of pleading when he tells me he knew she was going to her sister's house to watch episodes of Breaking Bad. He says he heard her tell me her plans as the two of them left the house last night, heard her tell me that she was taking Joey home, then headed to her sister's house.

I hear a whiney edge in my voice as I say, "You knew where she was going?" There's blood in the water, my young shark of a grandson senses it. He tells me;

"Mamo Kit," that's Joey's name for Laura's sister, *"Mamo Kit lives five minutes from here. You could have called or checked on her."*

Kid's got me. Try as I might, Joey won't side with me, but I'm not giving up easy.

Genuinely desperate now, I raise my voice to deliver, "She might have been in a ditch somewhere. Somebody might have knocked her on the head!" These are phrases I remember from my favorite detective novels. Like I said, I was desperate, but Joey wouldn't budge.

Finally, I say, "What if I stayed out all night?" I knew better. Never ask a question you don't know the answer to. Not in court and not when confronted by grandson.

"That is different," he replies. *"you are a child. For example, look at the kind of music you play. Real adults play classical music."*

There's no logic here, a child out all night is cause for alarm, but this doesn't stop him. Predator instinct on fire, my grandson sets-up for the kill;

"You have had a prolonged childhood. And now, you're through puberty but still just a teenager, mentally. My Dad is the same way."

Just like that, he delivers this last line knowing it's the clincher, the high ground on which he can safely rest his case. It just might be.

This response is so far from what I'd expected, for a few moments I'm stunned. Here we are - just my grandson and me, and I'm playing an admittedly juvenile game, taking advantage of this perfect opportunity to pick on girls. But the only juvenile in the tub, chronologically speaking, refuses to play along. Instead, he's gone all adult on me. The thing is, my reaction's totally out of proportion. I think my feeling are hurt. Me? Damn. No time for this, I must gather my wits!

But before my head clears I hear Joey say;

"Mankind may be the only species on earth that can truly be evil, or good."

Maybe this is his way of admitting that he's been a little hard on the old guy. Or, he may have realized that I'm thinking about holding his head underwater for as long as it takes to change his mind.

I admit his conversational topics are often loftier than mine. And he could be right about me being, childish. But all adults don't like classical music. My stepdad, for example was a rural American, man's man. He loved Country Western. Me? I'm gonna keep rock n' as long as I can.

Anyway, all this completely misses the point. I'm missing the point. Kit didn't call because there was nothing to worry about. Laura didn't call because she'd already told me what was up. And I wasn't really worried. I just got caught up with the idea of Joey and I playing head games with Laura, and didn't have the sense to let it go. Now I'd exposed myself as the butt of my own joke. Live and not learn, that's my style.

This never was just a silly, pick on the girl's game. It's about connecting with my grandson – sharing a joke and enjoying it for better reasons than how it scores on some maturity scale. Enjoying it because we'd have been doing it together. Doesn't matter how high-brow his conversation might be, he's not old enough to appreciate the importance of shared experiences. I'm the adult here, the one responsible for creating good memories and I'm not doing well.

Licking my wounded soul, I tell myself that I'm not sure I want to know the shenanigans that took place while I was practicing, I mean, being worried sick. This doesn't hold up. It's Laura we're talking about. I know better, but that doesn't stop me.

Whether brave or stupid, I give it a last try, saying, "Who knows what could have happened in those eight blocks, on the mean streets of La Grande, Oregon?"

Joey knows the answer. It's so obvious that he will not say it. Nothing would happen. Not a thing, unless Laura had decided to kick some guy's ass.

It has all been for good reasons, but I'd overplayed my hand.

Time to get out of the water.

BORN LUCKY

The hot tub? We still have it, but it's not new anymore. It's the same one you've been reading about. Joey Mallory is still our grandson, and he's still ten-years-old for a few more days. Just like in preceding episodes, as per his rules, Quiet Time is Joey's unscripted, stream of consciousness monologue. It's a speed rap that makes, mad-man, Electric Kool-Aid bus driver, Neal Cassady, look like Marcel Marceau.

When Joey's exploring fresh territory, cutting-edge material, his attention is on Laura. Those times when he wants to test the audience, his tone changes from wondrous speculation to something more like Spanish Inquisitor. These interrogations are directed at me.

When one of these assaults begins, I've learned to roll with it, just enjoy the ride. That way I'm less likely to suffer permanent injury. His intent is to maim, not kill. So, I proudly embrace my, Buffoon of the Family, status. This keeps the show funny, never boring.

The disturbing thing is that no one seems to realize that my part is just an act. This is shaping up like one of those times when the wise among us advise; "Don't ask unless you really want to know." Joey and Laura know it's just an act, Right?

So far, I've managed to swallow that question along with my suspicion of intentional humiliation. So far.

Tonight I'm off duty. Joey's working new material and Laura's getting all the attention. There's no photo so I can't prove it, but she's beginning to glow. Not knowing what was coming, I settled into the cheap seats to listen as he gets things started.

Retired now, Laura is still a registered nurse, at heart. Having worked as an obstetrics specialist for 35 years, she knows this stuff well. I'm sure she misses it.

Joey asked a question, a great one. He asked Laura how babies go from an aquatic environment to life outside the womb, breathing air. Now Laura totally lights up! It's like asking Ted Williams to tell you what he knows about connecting a bat with a speeding baseball. Without hesitation, she launches into a detailed explanation, at one point, jumping out of the tub and returning with a stack of 8X10's, circles and arrows on each one.

"Before birth, the lungs are not used," she explains. There's too much detail for me to quote precisely. But the condensed version is that the placenta carries oxygen and nutrients from the mother directly into the bloodstream of the fetus. Up until the time of birth, the baby's lungs are full of amniotic fluid. During birth, the mother's body produces hormones that cause its lungs to expel and absorb the fluids in preparation for the moment of delivery and the first breath.

Laura's excited and thoroughly enjoying herself and I'm engaged in her explanation when I hear Joey say;

"Mamo, I actually know the information. I just wanted to see if you were a good nurse."

I braced myself for what I was sure was coming. There are very few things that make this woman mad. But there is a specific list, at the top of which is being interrupted when she's in the middle of explaining something. Like now, when having been asked, she'd was delivering a lecture.

Everything stopped in the tub. Without even thinking about it, I move over, making room for an explosion. Staring at Joey, not saying a thing, she lets it sit there. Imagine my surprise and disappointment when after a couple of beats … she laughed!

Some guys have the knack.

MY PATIENT WIFE

Deep snow. Irish creme and coffee. Completely clear, cold winter sky. What a life! Who knew a guitar playing peckerwood, strum-bum of a musician could live in this fashion?

Laura and I are comfortable in silence. But we've grown used to Joey's monologue and without him, it felt too quiet. She didn't seem to want to talk all that much, so I made the most of a rare opportunity. Shouldering the responsibility of filling in for Joey, I spent the better part of an hour recounting my exploits - all of them. Past events that prove how cool I still am.

I should say, I was merely reminding her. After 40 years, I suspect she knows. But when it comes to some things, I do not mind offering a reminder, don't mind at all. Whether this was one of those times, that's open for discussion, but not now. As I said, Joey's absence has created an opportunity that I was not going to waste.

I've never heard another guy's routine. The details may change, but I'm guessing they follow a pattern.

"Then the bear jumped up and ran straight at me, as with steady hands, I chambered and fired the last round - hitting him right above the bridge of his nose. The monster dropped at my feet!"

On and on I talked. Laura, comforted by the knowledge that Joey would return, did a decent job of pretending to be interested.

Snow continued to fall.

What a life.

WEATHER AND A BIRTHDAY

It's already been an epic winter. The cold and snow have been unlike anything I've seen for years and we have a new president. Added to these, Joey turned eleven.

Late January now, late afternoon, early evening we're already in the tub and Joey's spinning our heads up with his philosophical musings. Laura and I listen to him and watch the sky as the stars begin to blink on.

Joey thought it was amazing that every age you reach seems like the perfect age. Except for thirteen. He tells us;

"...thirteen seems like the really perfect, ideal age. You are a teenager and that is cool. You have some life experience - you know some stuff. No one has high expectations of you, so your responsibilities are limited. You have more freedom. You have one foot in the past and one foot in the present. The future is still a long way away."

He delivers all this without a pause or hesitation. And yes, it has required Laura's good memory to help me recreate his entire speech.

As you can tell, he'd thought it through. It was

quite a list. I was convinced, thirteen is perfect. And so far, it was all harmless. Interesting, but harmless. That was about to change. Intuition or experience, I knew something was coming.

His gaze landed on me as he observed;

"It seems like Mallory men do not evolve after the age of thirteen. I hope to break that mold."

This caught me totally flat-footed, unprepared. I tried to defend myself, to no avail. My protests must have sounded as hollow as they felt. Expecting that she would, to my surprise, Laura didn't leap to my defense. Quite the reverse, she seemed amused. Just when you begin to think they really love you…

Already up to my neck in dark waters, I took another step. "Give me an example of my, thirteen-year-old, behavior," I said. Without a moment of hesitation, he says;

"You're a crybaby."

Turning to Laura, he caps his retort with;

"Isn't he!" Declarative, not a question.

Knowing she was walking a fine line she chose her words carefully. Because I've been trying to forget the incident, I can't quote her. What I remember is that she never said, "No, he is not a crybaby."

Joey showered and got ready to go home. Anytime I suggested he speed it up or ask if he had his backpack and homework, he said;

"You are such a crybaby."

As we were leaving, I'm quite sure I heard Laura say, "It's gonna be cold outside, don't be a crybaby." She said it under her breath from behind me as we walked to the truck. I'm pretending that she was talking to Joey.

The distance to Joey's house is little more than a mile, just a few minutes, not even long enough to warm up the engine. It really is cold but I'm not saying a word.

After delivering my tormentor to his doorstep, we head back to our house. The ride back is quiet.

Joey's home and warm. That's all either of us really cared about.

GRASSHOPPER SPINS

Joey's world is expanding as it should. Unfortunately, this means that he's no longer coming to our house every day. In with the new and out with the old. A natural progression, evolution on the micro scale. I'm getting carried away here, he's just growing up.

Although his visits are slightly less frequent, he continues to come over when he has homework to do. Homework is still followed by Quiet Time in the tub. These days, his commentary is a mixture of Neil Tyson-Degrasse and H. D. Thoreau. Don't get me wrong, there are plenty of not-so intellectual musings too. He does wild rant's, great stuff that reminds me of Don Rickles. Yesterday's entertainment began before the actual tubbing took place.

Knowing that Joey loves Shel Silverstein, Laura had ordered three, large hardbound, Silverstein books. The books arrived but Laura wasn't home when Joey showed up. Joey had homework so here he was at our house. Seeing the books, he said;

"Mamo is totally buttering me up because she misses me."

I see an angle here. Meantime, he loved the books, and after thanking her when she returned he finished his homework and we all headed for the tub.

This is when I tell Laura what Joey had said. They both shrugged, and she agreed. Laura had hoped the books would encourage more visits. Still, I was hoping Joey would at least get a lecture. So much for my angle.

Things did get better for me. Seeing that Joey had deeply disappointed Laura, I could not have been happier. Some shake their heads at what passes for love at our house. We just laugh.

Next, Joey tells us that Curly is hilarious. Disappointment forgotten, this is a conversation I could understand. The Stooges - all three of them. I told Joey that Curly was my favorite as a child but as I matured, Larry took the top spot. He was, by far the funniest and best-looking stooge, in my opinion.

Conversation quieted as Joey began to read Silverstein aloud. He's a great reader and likes to read to an audience. Fearless. After showering, the Stooges and the Curly conversation resurfaced, sort of. Without saying a word, Joey drops to the floor and does a Curly Spin. No words needed, I'm happy to be proven wrong.

Forget what I said about Larry, Curly is the funniest stooge. My chest swelled with pride.

Yes, we are going to bribe him to visit us. Yes, we irritate his parents. Yes, they set limits with us. Yes, they are both great parents. Yes, they are very generous with Joey. They never, well, seldom tell us no.

Joey knows the value of the Curly Spin. I've done all I can. No longer a grasshopper, with that spin he has snatched the pebble from my hand.

We will see Joey less and less. He has a life.

All is right in the universe.

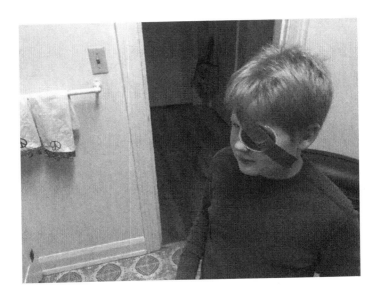

UNLOCKED

Joey has a couple of pals in the neighborhood that knock on the door to see if he is at our house. The boys play in our large backyard. Laura and I enjoy the noise, orders for food and general mayhem.

Joey plays with all the tools from the shed. As it happened, I looked out the back window as he and one of his buddies were playing some version of mumblety-peg with the chopping mall.

For those who don't remember: The game requires at least two players. The first takes out his pocket knife and throws it, attempting to stick the blade in the ground as close as possible to his own foot. The next player does the same. The one who sticks his knife closest to his foot wins.

But you could win on the first throw if you were unlucky or crazy enough to stick the knife directly into your own foot. What can I say? This was a time before cell phones and stuff. Kids needed something to do.

Fast forward, forty years; boys have traded in their pocket knives for cell phones to keep up with the girls. This effectively put an end to mumblety-peg and the fun of playing with sharp objects. At least, until Joey found our maul.

This brings us to today's subject. The two boys in my backyard didn't own a pocket knife between the pair of them, so they went big. Like I said, they were using a mall - a ten-pound sledgehammer with an ax blade on one end. Just the ticket!

I knew they were not aiming at their feet, no matter, this would have sent me to the moon when I was a young parent. With steam coming out of my ears, I'd have lectured and changed the lock on the shed. I would have been a thundering pain in the ass.

These days, I take another sip of coffee, shrug and think to myself, "A kid has to learn."

Feeling lofty, I liken it to accepting the laws of nature. Sometimes this means respecting the unique talents of others.

Some of us let kids drink coffee and run near the edge of the cliff. Others are better at being disciplinarians.

Having staked out the high ground, I let Laura do the adult thing. She's a great playground monitor, her performance in this instance proving the point. With just a few words, apparently the right ones, she pulled it off perfectly.

No one argued. Nobody was embarrassed.

The shed remains unlocked.

THE PROTEST

Laura has a cold and Joey has decided to spend this weekend with us. Feeling less than well, Laura has not been able to cater to his every whim. Joey handled this hideous turn of events like a trooper. He let Laura sleep and began work on a dinosaur painting that will cover one of our walls. Yesterday he finished the head. It looks awesome.

While Laura was recovering, and Michelangelo was working on our new living room mural, I left the house headed for my store. In my mind, this meant I was going to work. I say this specifically because I've been accused of running a clubhouse. Meaning that time spent at my store is not real work, not a job that makes real money.

In my defense, I remind them that, in fact, my clubhouse pays very well. This reasoning changes nothing. Knowing it irritates me, the clubhouse accusation has taken on a life of its own and my family will never let it go. It's a strategy I taught them. Once you sense weakness, never let up. Always keep the other guy off balance. It's a family thing.

The clubhouse joke stems from the fact that I'm a working musician who's owned a music store for thirty-five years. The store is kind of Fifty's style, with a few things on the shelves and hanging on the walls that haven't moved for years. Between these museum pieces sits the rest of the inventory. If it's related to music, we have it.

Customers and friends drift in and out all day. The cash register and credit card machines hum along steadily as people catch up or stay current, exchanging stories about those who aren't there to defend themselves. All in all, a pretty relaxed atmosphere, but still a business, or so I thought. Others disagree. It's not the clubhouse label that gets me. It's the insinuation that I don't work for a living.

Writing this has given me an idea. I think I'll have cards printed - membership cards. Anybody who comes in and presents one of these cards gets it punched, no purchase necessary. Once cardholders realize that it's not worth a damn, it'll die out. But while the idea is still hot, Joey and Laura will be denied membership. Never let the game go stale!

Added to running the store and playing in a band, I perform solo, which is how this episode gets started.

A couple of weeks ago my one-man show had been requested. The event happened yesterday, a rally opposing talk in Washington about repealing the Affordable Care Act. Everybody knows that the current system has problems. I just have reservations about President Trump's ability to fix them. And I don't want the most vulnerable among us to suffer. To be fair, I'm sure that nobody wants that. But back to the story, which once again leads us to the hot tub.

Joey's love for the tub has never dimmed. Last night, about 10:00 pm, he came bounding into the living room and excitedly yelled two words;

"COME! NOW!"

I did as I was told. Lid off, water steaming, jets squirting - he has the tub ready for the two of us. All I had to do was put on a swimsuit to comply with another one of his rules;

"Nobody is free-wheeling in here. That would be creepy!"

Settling into the water, the curtains rise on Quiet Time and we're all ears for another episode of, The Joey Show! This reminds me of an old commercial. Re-purposed, it would now read; "When Joey speaks, people listen." It was a pitch for one of the big investment brokerages. I figure we're investing in Joey.

Breaking the rules, I told him about me playing

my first protest gig in forty-five years, yesterday. I had been asked to sing one of my favorite Woody Guthrie's songs, This Land Is Your Land. Woody Guthrie, I'll show up and sing anything of his, this one in particular, for anybody.

But I told him there was something about the deal that bothered me. When I arrived, I found out that the organizers had written new lyrics to suit the occasion. Before I'd even seen their revision, I didn't like it. I told Joey the whole story.

Instead of not shushing me, he was quiet and had his head tilted back looking at the sky. I assumed he was not listening at all. Lowering his head, he caught my eye and said;

"I am going to miss winter in the hot tub. The cold, clear, dark blue sky filled with stars and the bright moon reflecting on the snow, make night bright as day."

He hadn't been listening to me, and yes, I was offended. But thinking about what I'd said left me feeling small. Now, convinced that he had not heard a word I'd said, I was thankful that my trifling concerns had not registered.

Au contraire! He'd heard every word - heard me rave about how Guthrie came to write that particular song, heard me say that I did not like it when anyone twists an iconic tune to support an agenda. He'd heard me say it was lame for anybody to use the strength of a great song to drive another message. I'd be critical of those on the Right or Left for doing such a thing.

Turning his head to look at me, he said;

"The reason it bothers you is that, no matter what you think of the President, this is his land too."

Joey looked back up into space, and the world was quiet.

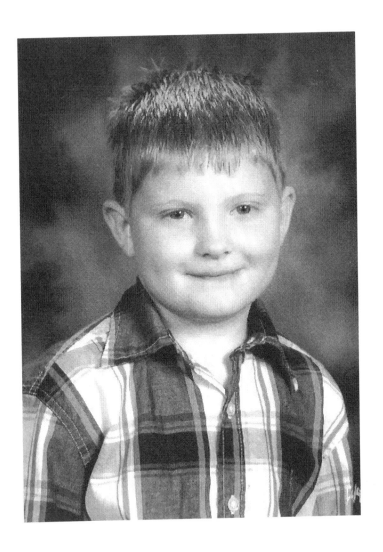

ROBERTO DURAN

When Lara bought the hot tub, I did not realize that we had that much extra money. Proof positive, we live in a pretty cool country, a guy like me reaping the benefits of a place Woody Guthrie called, The Pastures of Plenty. Not bad!

Joey visits us less regularly these days. He comes over if he has homework or if he's in the mood for some tub time. Quiet Time. I love the total travesty he's made of those words. After all these months he still talks continuously, and I still think he's interesting.

The last couple of weeks have been great for Joey. It's Fall already, and he's enrolled in a private school, a difficult, no-nonsense one. Their day starts at 8:00 AM and ends at 3:00. The classrooms are orderly, and the front office staff knows what is happening to every student, all the time. The curriculum includes P.E., music and a healthy amount of outdoor play. It's still called, recess. I don't know why, but this surprises me.

This school does not give awards unless you actually achieve something. High marks for the school, and according to the report-card he just got, high marks for Joey too - nearly straight A's. He didn't get one for Penmanship or Chapel.

In a previous chapter, I made a fuss about us not being a religious family. Now Joey's attending a Christian school. His parents simply saw it as the best option, academically. As a family, we all agree that irreverence is one of the higher art forms. But that's got nothing to do with the kids getting a great education.

So, Joey's teacher told Laura that he reads his Bible verse on Monday, memorizes it and never looks at it again. Students are tested on Friday. Sometimes Joey doesn't remember exactly how the verse is worded, but he understands the message and can explain it. I think this is great! However, that was not the assignment. No, "A," for Joey.

He did get an award, his second in as many weeks. And as I said, awards aren't given without good reason. I don't have the certificate in front of me, but it said things about exemplary behavior. His teacher, herself top-notch, says Joey had been outstanding for the last couple weeks. Regarding this second weekly award, Joey says;

"Usually sequels are inferior. In my case, two is just as good as one."

Yes, he could use some help with his sentence structure. And no, humility is not his strong suit.

More important, I do not ⟨
this boy.

Last night's hot tub, ⟨
at least for me. It inⲥ⟨
understanding how people cⲟ⟨
And that it would be easy ⲓⲟ
children. He says this explains why dictaⲟ⟨
on the young. I don't know what, or whⲓⲥ
dictator he's referring to, but I agree when he
says;

"Young kids are vulnerable," he reasons, *"and
want to please."*

He singles out elementary school-aged kids,
saying that those his age and younger tend to
believe what they are told by adults, those in
authority. All but Joey, it seems.

Not finished, he informs me that;

*"Adults just want a good life for their family.
Poverty and hunger are powerful tools. You listen
when your stomach speaks."*

His monologue nearly over, Joey wound it up by
letting me know that he does not feel vulnerable
to poverty and hunger, and how lucky he feels,
knowing he was getting a good education.

me.

recently watched a biographical movie ... Roberto Duran. Duran, the great boxer m the 1970s through the 90s. This brought to mind how Sugar Ray Leonard and Muhammad Ali stole rounds. Meaning, they would coast for the first couple of minutes and then throw a flurry of punches as the clock was ticking down toward the end, thus stealing the round on the scorecards.

Joey's parent-teacher conference is coming up. Not meaning to be cynical, though it does come easy, I wondered if his stellar behavior at school is his version of stealing rounds? An award or two just before his Mom and Dad talk to the teacher might be the ticket.

Chuckling, I keep this revelation to myself and drift back into Joey's orbit in time to hear him say;

"We cannot hate each other because of the way we vote. Everybody wants what is best for their family."

I snickered, and said, "Sure, round-stealer." Joey stopped short, and we experienced a rare moment of silence in the tub.

He knows that I have a convoluted but accurate

way of connecting things. Realizing that he had no idea what I was talking about and sensing that curiosity would not serve him well, he let it go. So did I. My explanation would ruin his Quiet Time.

He thinks that award pulled him across the line, that he's taken the round on points. Considering that he's completely unaware of what I've figured out, I score this one as a win for me, a knockout.

Kid' never knew what hit him!

THE BIG SLEEP

Joey has been gone for a week. He's in Vancouver, Washington. My oldest son, Kevin and his wife live there with their two boys. He spends as much vacation time as possible with Kevin and family.

Before leaving, Joey had discovered Columbo, Peter Falk's classic TV detective character. Columbo has worked his way into Joey's speed-raps. He loved how the detective would irritate his suspects, keeping them off balance with his questions and odd timing.

Predictably, Joey began to mimic the star's signature line. "Just one more thing," he'd say in his Columbo voice. Then to our amazement, he'd shift subjects, moving his one-man, stream of consciousness show forward, stringing the nights' succession of topics together. By the end it seemed that everything was part of a believably related whole.

At some point, he picked up on a conversation Laura and I were having. He was not used to us flapping our gums as he was pondering life, but stayed quiet, absorbing the details of our slightly hushed conversation.

We were talking about my Dad. For the past several

years he's been sliding deeper into dementia. The word from the other side of the family is that my Dad is not expected to live much longer. So, Laura and I were whispering about death. Guess what? Joey has a view! Among other things, he tells us;

"... nobody is really ever, GONE. Everybody carries the people they love with them all the time, dead or alive."

Where does he get this stuff?

He said he would always carry Mamo with him. Mamo is what he has always called Laura. Joey was looking at me the entire time he was talking about the grim reaper. Assuming my role as the family stooge, I ask, "So how about me?" Kid didn't miss a beat;

"Nah, we'll all forget about you in a couple of days." He replied.

Laughter ensued. Except for Laura.

Joey had gone from the highest of highs to the lowest position a Mallory male can fall, launching Laura into a lecture. Behavior was the theme. Respect and Courtesy were primary elements of her plot. Comedy for me. A dark story for Joey.

As I've said before, we're a, Live and Let Live, tribe. Still, there are rules - lines in the sand. To Laura's way of thinking, Joey had crossed a big one. I kept my mouth shut, didn't even chuckle. Very much. Joey wasn't laughing at all.

Later, in part to help him regain his composure, I told Joey how my Dad got me interested in detectives. An avid reader, Dad didn't just read detective novels, but they were a respected part of the mix. He introduced me to Travis McGee, Spenser, Elvis Cole, all the gumshoes from the 1920s thru to present day writers. All the characters created by the genres best authors.

I told him his great-grandfather would like him. "The reason," I tell him, "You're self-contained. You don't break stuff," I said. "And you only ask questions that need asking. Your interaction with him would be interesting." Taking it further I said, "He'd like the fact that you research stuff and don't talk about things you don't already know something about. You're comfortable in your own skin, comfortable being alone. You even remind me of my Dad."

I was piling it on pretty thick, but it was all true. And Joey was back! He asked me to order the box-set so we could have a weekend marathon. I did, so now we've got it. But Columbo will have to wait.

No more than a week has passed since our conversation and I'm driving West on I-84. Early that morning I got the call. My father has died. Clearing the deck for funeral arrangements, I'll bring Joey and Kevin's boys back to our place. I'm meeting Kevin halfway between La Grande and Vancouver. The mid-point is Arlington, a town on the Oregon side of the Columbia River.

Now on the turn-around, three boys and me in a car. There are still a couple of hundred miles to cover and hamburgers to eat. I could not be depressed if I tried. That should be my epitaph. I would have sworn it was 1985 and I was taking my own three boys on a trip. There is no better therapy for the hole death leaves than the activity of the living.

Once again, Joey's right. You carry your loved ones with you all the time, dead or alive. I am also right. My Dad would have really liked Joey.

He'd have enjoyed him the same as Laura and I do. Connections in the gene pool are obvious. I know that he would have laughed out loud when Joey said, *"... we will all forget about you in a couple of days."*

As I was mulling over these seemingly random but related thoughts I heard my grandson say,

"...that is how democracies fail."

I don't know what this conversational fragment connects to. Next, I chuckled hearing him wonder why anyone would put lemons on a pizza, having seen Uncle Kevin eating a slice topped with pineapple.

So, I guess what all this means is;

Do whatever it takes to be happy every minute and never say goodbye.

It's not necessary.

100

MOTHER'S DAY

There is still a hot tub in my backyard. Joey, now eleven, is still noisy during Quiet Time. After all this time, I've never busted him, never confronted him about how loud he is when he's being "quiet." Why spoil the fun? So, when Joey talks, we listen.

When Joey comes over, he brings his energy in the door. Sincerity and clarity, they must be two of the secrets of the universe. These and a general love of life radiate from him, making the whole house feel brighter. I'm sure we're not the first grandparents who've ever felt this way. We stand in awe and bathe in his presence.

On this most recent hot tub day, Laura and I had an argument. An honest to goodness, yell fight. This is something Joey has never seen us do. He was highly amused. He rarely laughs out loud but did this time. Hearing us bicker didn't traumatize him. Instead, he thought it was hilarious.

We were arguing because of the weeds in our backyard. Laura had decided that we were no longer going to use Weed N' Feed, Round Up or any other similar products. Eco-Friendly was her conjoined word of the day, and Eco-Friendly products would be used. Some sort of corn product on the lawn and around the patio. Good thing we don't have cockroaches. I'm pretty sure they find this stuff nutritious. Cornmeal, salt, and vinegar. Oh yeah, she's adding a little dish soap. I guess that's supposed to insure a clean kill.

Laura said she could dig up anything that didn't die after exposure to this Eco-Sensitive punishment. I lobbied for the tried and true method, petrochemical refinery waste. If that fails, nuke-em! Raising the level of her voice to a new high, she nuked me.

Both of us tend to be bossy. Still, we rarely disagree. But this Weed N' Feed fight led to us yelling full throttle. All this in front of Joey, who thought it was awesome!

I gave in. The argument ended, and we retired to the hot tub.

Now it was funny to Laura and me too. We were all chuckling about the fight. Laura said she was glad we stopped when we did. She didn't want it to explode into domestic violence. This got a huge laugh. Joey looked at me and said;

"I know you would never hit Mamo. I am not as sure about the reverse."

This also got a huge laugh. We can laugh because violence in our house is unthinkable.

Joey asked me if I was willing to use products that might give my grandchildren cancer just to have a luscious lawn. I had to admit that I was indeed willing to do such a thing. Laura and Joey looked at each other and shook their heads in disgust.

One of the results of our yelling match was that it made deciding on the perfect Mother's Day gift very easy. I got Laura her own, hand-powered weed remover. The old school, fork looking tool. I grew up on the wrong end of one that looked just like it. And I'm going to have her name burned into the handle. Nothing is too good for the mother of my children and life partner.

Yes, it was Mother's Day, but I got Joey a gift too, a Saint Christopher's medal on a silver chain. His name is engraved on the back. I'm not a Catholic, not even religious unless you stretch the definition. But as a teenager, I wore one given to me. I liked it, liked the idea. I still do. The thought of a Saint watching things seems like a good idea for Joey too.

Move'n and shake'n, Joey is making his way, traveling through life. I hope he likes the pendant and feels what I did, finds the same unexplainable ease that I always had when I put it on.

Happy Mother's Day to all of you who qualify.

Find the ones you need and keep them close. Or give them a Saint Chris medal.

Maybe, like for Joey, do both.

THE CONFESSION

Joey has found other things to fill his time besides hanging out with his grandparents. This change was expected, one of those natural progressions, as required for a healthy life. Still, it kinda sucks. However, he still drops by to visit and touch base, like today.

Joey's running another monologue. Words come fast and coherent, as though scripted and displayed in front of his eyes. All this, of course, takes place in the hot tub, where on this particular afternoon he's speculating on how sound might be the unseen force that keeps everything in place in the universe.

"This is the explanation of dark matter," he tells us.

Not surprisingly, he did not ask for my input. His theory was birthed full form, no need of help from me. No need for help from long departed, Albert Einstein, or the ghost of Richard Feynman either. I think he's convinced that none of us could contribute anything meaningful. Einstein and Feynman remained silent, so why should I stick my nose in? I didn't.

Out for the summer - the private school he attends released students around the third week of May, so Joey's free to arrange things, and arrange things, he did. He's headed back to Vancouver, to Uncle Kevin's house to resume his visit. Even with two boys of their own, Kevin and his wife Jessica always welcome Joey with open arms. Kevin's kids, Jackson and Kaleb, are younger than Joey. Still, the three of them are tight. Joey likes these visits because in his words;

"I can just be a kid."

So … what is he when he's not with his cousins? That's a little scary. One more question I don't want to ask.

Before leaving town, he made a series of drawings. Several looked like prehistoric birds with armor. While he was discussing his work with Laura, I detected an opening. I'm usually quiet during his hot tub musings. Not this time.

Done in pencil, the drawings were detailed. Now Joey wants Mamo, Laura to color them while he's gone. I asked him if he thought coloring was a girl's job. I knew I had him. This admission would not sit well with Laura. He was in so much trouble!

Joey asked me why and how I arrived at such a conclusion. I countered with, "Who colors the best in your class." Joey rattled off a few names.

All of them the monikers of girls in his grade. Before I could hammer him on that point, he said;

"Maybe that is how people your age think. I just think Mamo colors better than I do."

A clear case of defeat snatched from the jaws of victory. Topping it off, until now I have never thought of Joey as a liar. This moment has changed my opinion of him. Trust has been shoved down the dark hole of doubt. That's how it felt in the moment, knowing he'd tricked me. This has become a dark matter. Dark energy courses through my brain.

What to do?

I've never thought torture was a good thing, the right way for the governments or anyone else, for that matter, to obtain a confession. Now I'm thinking that this might have been the mental voice of inexperience speaking.

I've been ruminating on this conversation, what I'd come to believe was Joey's lie, for a couple of weeks. It makes me feel small. Days go by and still this episode. His treachery is stuck in my craw. Which may explain recurring thoughts of torture I've been having.

I'm not saying that I'll use the technique, but does

anyone know how to waterboard?

DOES HE KNOW?

Public school and an extra hour on the bus each day. These and new friends had taken more of Joey's time these past few months. But as May ended, so did classes. Meaning, it's summer vacation.

Joey has resumed his near-daily visits and Quiet Time. We had missed him and now welcomed the increased frequency. I like to think that we are not clingy, but suspect we would be if we thought we could get away with it.

Time in the tub varies with the seasons. Colder months find us in the water at earlier hours. Now it's summer, a hot, long, wonderful summer, and an invitation to late night soaking. Following the heat of mid-day, the evenings are pleasantly cool. The sky is deep blue, and stars abound. Plus the big one for an eleven-year-old; No school in the morning!

Joey's spent a lot of time at our house over the years. Late nights in the tub make sleepovers practical for everyone.

Often a last-minute decision, he calls home to ask for permission. This does not work every time, but his parents usually say yes, which pleases us. By now that must be obvious.

Maybe we need to get a life?

No, this is my life. Laura, Joey, and the band.

Being a musician, I often get home really late. Summer. No school. Rolling all this together makes for interesting but odd time in the tub. A case in point, the band had played another show out of town and it was after midnight when I walked through the front door.

To Joey, the situation presented the possibility of high adventure. I'd little more than laid my head on the pillow when I heard his voice in the dark.

"The hot tub," he was telling me.

Long day, hard night and me almost asleep.

"Come get in the tub!" he said a second time.

To the water we went. Laura joined us, and it was perfect. Carpe Noctem!

Like all families, from time to time, like now, we were working through some challenges. Which explains our conversation during this early morning soak-session. Joey had been talking about how different members of our family handle anger, stress, and sadness. Laura was assuring him that everything was going to be okay.

Expanding, she went on to say how impressed she was that he has such insight on so many topics. But smart as she is, she also told him, "Be a kid. Let adults be adults. It's their job to work things out." Again, she assured him, "Everything's going to be fine."

In recent years, I've had trouble with my vision. Even so, near blind as I am, I could see two blue beams, the lasers that was given for eyes are focused on me. Up to that point, I'd tried to stay out of it. The conversation had been for the adults in the tub. My character in this theater troupe is not one of them. This is supposed to be funny, and the background for much of our comedy. Plus, it served me well that night. Tired as I was, I didn't feel like participating.

The things Laura had said must have had the right effect. Feeling more like himself, he decides that I needed inclusion. Speaking to Laura, he said;

"Peapa handles problems by burying them. Then he buries the shovel. I think he suffers from an Object-Permanence disorder."

Between chuckles, Laura agreed. Next, he asked.

"Does Peapa know what that means"?

I see nothing to gain by revealing her answer.

I do bury stuff. And I've planted plenty of shovels. But here I sit in the early morning hours with my wife and a kid who can open me faster than a can of coke. He's nailed me with the Object-Permanence accusation. I have no idea what it means, if it means anything at all. Either way, it's all small-change compared to the pleasure I'm feeling being here with these two.

After a long day and nights work, neck deep in hot water with two of the people I care about the most in this world. They're laughing and making fun of me. No matter. I couldn't have been more at peace.

Object-Permanence? What I know is, the time is coming when Joey is not going to want to sit in a tub of hot water at three in the morning with a creepy old man. "Enjoy it while you can," I'm thinking. The object is to accept impermanence.

I think I understand a few things they're reluctant to give me credit for. Like the fact that if I were the type to think too much about everything it means to see Joey growing up, it could make me sad. But that's not me. What come's later will just have to come later. For now, I'm going to soak, groove and smile.

Another thing I know is that being with my wife and listening to this kid so late at night that it's already morning, I'm at the center of everything worthwhile in the universe. Even the memory makes me shake my head in wonder.

Oh, just so you know, I looked up Object Permanence. Tack on, "Disorder," and Joey really did nail it. Burying problems, I'm good at it. But long term, it never worked very well.

Wherever I am I *see* Laura and Joey in living color. Even though they are not with me, I know they are real. Maybe I'm cured!

HOUSE RULES

Joey has spent a fair amount of time around adults. Maybe this is why he's not shy about making up rules that suit him. Like his ridiculous declaration that hot tub time must be quiet.

For me it is quiet. I mean, I'm quiet, Joey's not. I rarely speak a single word. When I do, it's just as seldom factored into his monologue.

That's another indication of his confidence. Right or wrong, he's comfortable with his ideas. Somewhere between him being a bright kid and the fact that I'm his grandfather, it's all working. But it's Joey coming up with new rules that figures in here. We will get to that soon enough.

There's been a changed in the house. Joey's cousins have moved back to town. Counting Joey, these three are staggered in age like my three sons. My own, not the old TV show. Their ages are eleven, ten and eight. Joey, Jax, (short for Jackson), and Kaleb. Also like my sons, they are close.

We provide daycare for the three of them. But that sounds almost clinical. What I mean is that with school out for the summer, the boys are at or somewhere around our place during the day.

Nighttime too, if the parents allow the boys to sleep-over. They're easy to have around, considering that we enjoy the mayhem.

I say this in-spite of the fact that Laura and I are watching a food bill gone sky high. I didn't remember how much three growing boys could consume. Someday, when I've run out of meaningful work, I want to look into connections between the anti-contraception lobby and grocery stores. Anyway, on with the story.

Apparently, Joey had taken note of the chaos resulting from three kids and two adults in one small house. I'm confident of this because during our latest soaking adventure he announced that we needed some rules. "House and bathroom rules," he tells us.

Rule-making and enforcement are not my strong suit. Honestly, I would not know where to begin. Joey had no problem quickly dictating his rules to Laura. I was not consulted. Maybe it was just the fact that I was at work …okay, at the clubhouse. Either way, news leaked. I could hardly wait to get home and hear all of the new policies.

We had rules when our boys were young but never a list. Certainly, never a House and Bathroom rule distinction. Laura agreed to every one of them. She probably did it knowing I'd find the whole thing hilarious. But I'm not letting her off the hook, not yet. I'm sticking with, "Laura agreed to every one of them."

So, Joey is convinced that we need some law and order around here now that the population has almost doubled. The statutes are unambiguous, to the point of overly ridged. No matter, Laura was right, they're hilarious. With her operating behind the scenes they may even have been written for me. I'm not sure about this, but I am suspicious.

I'm looking at the equivalent of Moses' stone tablets. Two pages - two handwritten lists. Joey's work, no mistake. The first, predictably titled; "House Rules," hangs in the living room. The second; "Bathroom Rules," is on display in the bathroom. Where else? Here they are:

HOUSE RULES

1. Shoes At Door
2. No Cussing
3. Close Doors
4. No Whining
5. No Cry Whining (There is a difference.)
6. No Talk Back
7. No Micro Managing (My Fav!)

8. Hands To Self - If Harm Is Meant
9. Clean Your Mess
10. No Arguing

BATHROOM RULES

1. Do Not Bring Electronics Into Bathroom
2. Do Not Make A Mess
3. Close The Toilet
4. FLUSH (Notice, he wrote this one, all-caps.)
5. Open The Window
6. WASH AND DRY HANDS (Also, all-caps.)

No electronics in the bathroom? I'm not sure if it's the slim possibility of being electrocuted by a TV remote or the fact that he's a bit of a germaphobe, but it freaks him out. No matter, now they're outlawed!

House Rules? Bathroom Rules? I want - no, I need to laugh, but I play it straight. They have won. This state of affairs is stunning, a resounding and humiliating defeat for me.

Stomping my inner feet for all to see the pain of my surrender, I let it be known that I can adjust and follow all the rules, except one:

I will NEVER give up Cry Whining. I'm in charge around here, not Joey or Laura!

I think Laura will agree with this, knowing as she does that it's not true, the "in charge," part.

I'm not so sure about Joey.

Okay, I know he won't.

SOUL EDITION

Like I've explained, I play in a band with my son, Joey's Dad. When we're playing out of town, Joey hangs out with Laura.

Summer is our busy season. It's late July and this month has been crazy busy. We've been playing three or more nights a week and rarely in town. We drive an average of a hundred miles, set-up and play the gig. Then we tear down, pack-up and drive home. Keep this in mind the next time you're tempted to chant and cheer until your favorite band plays an encore set. Much of this paragraph sounds like Cry Whining, which is inappropriate. We're a band, fer-chrissake. We love it! All I needed to say is that I get home late.

This is another story that starts on one of those early mornings after an exhausting night. I've just pulled to a stop in my driveway. Trying to be quiet, I close the pickup door softly, and carefully lift my guitar case out of the back of the truck. Looking at my watch as I opened the door, it was 3:30 am. Still, stepping inside, I was not all that surprised to see a head pop up on the couch like a jack in the box. Joey was awake.

Limping across the living room, I'd just sat my guitar on the floor and myself in my chair when the blitzkrieg began. He wanted me to make a sandwich for him. A very specific sandwich – ham on a French roll with American cheese. Joey reminds me that twenty-nine seconds is the perfect amount of time to nuke this culinary taste treat. How did he arrive at this conclusion? This was not his first ham and cheese melt. He makes them for himself all the time. He could make this one.

No matter; To Joey, tonight, this morning, I'm his designated chef. Big matter to me, I can hardly move. My legs were aching, I'm exhausted and here's my grandson sucker punching my psyche. I can't help but chuckle at this combination of intensity and innocence. The kids only eleven and has no idea what, "deep fatigue" means. No clue as to how I feel.

Not wanting to move let alone make his sandwich, I try a little diversion. I ask him why he's awake this late. Doesn't work, he doesn't budge. Round One goes to Joey.

Hope comes from an unexpected direction. The truck, the front door, and our voices did it. We'd woken Laura. I take aim, and with pleasure, bring this news to his attention. As the round's ending, I've landed a shot that shut him up! But only momentarily. His hungry, expectant eyes speak for him, and they are still focused - no, they're riveted on me. Round Two is a draw.

Round Three. In an act of pure subterfuge, I told him I would make his sandwich if he would massage my legs, knowing exactly how creepy that request happens to be. I loved my Grandpa Mallory more than I can describe, but there is no way on God's green earth I would have massaged his bony, lumpy, blue-veined, white as a frog's belly legs. Not when I was eleven. Not even now!

Joey stood in front of me with his hands stretched out uncertainly. His face held a combined look of puzzlement and nausea, like I'd stuck a plate of something mysterious but rotten smelling under his nose. I've connected again. He lowers his arms and I'm doubly relieved. If he'd attempted the leg massage it would not have been a relaxing experience, and his sandwich idea is off the table. The judges scribble. The cards are raised. Round Three is mine!

As artfully as I've managed to erase my name from the midnight line-cook roster, Joey demonstrates an equally masterful, face-saving move of his own. Pivoting gracefully, he says;

"Let's take a hot tub!"

It's now well after 4 am, and the three of us are in the tub as the bell rings and round four begins. Joey's been stargazing then lowers his eyes to say;

"There are things that feed your soul and things that rob your soul."

Out of nothing more than habit, a snarky, smart-mouthed comment came to mind and began the short trip from thought to spoken words. I've never been shy about saying whatever it takes to convince myself that I'm the funniest guy in the room, another habit that doesn't serve me well.

But a wise young man had just told me that there are things that feed your soul, and things that rob your soul. Suspecting that this applies to what I was about to deliver... I said nothing.

Friends, family, anyone who knows me will tell you that I don't let people tell me what to do or say. Nobody except for Laura and this kid who's less and less of a kid these days.

Those snarky words and the impulse to deliver them were still there. An impulse powered by years of practice has stalled-out halfway. It's now a lump in my throat. A senseless remark restrained by the wisdom of my grandson. The same one who'd recently tried to manipulate a tired man into making him a sandwich in the middle of the night.

"Feed or rob your soul," He'd said.

I swallowed. The lump, words and all, went down. I think they fed my soul.

Thanks to my grandson, maybe this one time, I got it right.

Forget the judges, I give Round Four to Joey.

COME WITH ME KID

Joey's uncle Jesse came to town a couple of weeks ago. He's a contractor in the big city. Successful as his migration has been, he's a country boy at heart.

Our family has passed a treasure down through the generations, a cabin in the middle of the woods. One hundred twenty acres of mountain woodlands bordering a wilderness area. Paradise. A perfect place for a man in need of relief from Metro Madness.

Jesse took Joey to the cabin. They built a fire pit. They hiked. They worked on the place, and Joey learned to drive, all the things a kid can do in the woods. The best part is that he got to hang out with his uncle for a week just doing things. Things that we forget are important until we return to paradise.

There's a bridge on the cabin property. All Mallory boys have been, or must go under the bridge. Totally tribal, it's our rite of passage. "Going under," means wading ice-cold, thigh-high water, slippery rocks and all. Added to the cold, the bridge is wide, and dark underneath.

Great for young boys, it still creeps me out.

Now I learn that Joey upped the ante. He added to the challenge. Adding dark to darkness, he did it at night. Why didn't I think of that? The bar has been raised, and Joey makes sure that his Dad and uncles know all about it.

The best part of this week was that I realized Joey, not unlike his Uncle Jesse, is a good guy. Let me explain.

Jesse had also invited two long-time friends, now married, to join them for the first couple of nights. They brought Richard, their five-year-old son who I dubbed, Little Richard. Sensing that he has just met a new hero, Little Richard acted as though he was in the presence of James Dean, Bogart or Brando. Choosing a name from the current, alpha-male pantheon, Richard chose Joey.

Not the shy type, Little Richard had asked Jesse to introduce the two of them. All this happened before they left for the cabin so I was there watching, not sure how this would go down. Joey can be stand-offish, at least I've seen it directed toward adults. Not so in this case. Responding to Jesse's request, Joey did more than just show his new friend around. He took him under his wing, taught him some moves.

Shirtless, sunglasses, and the St. Christopher's

medal I'd given him, hanging on his chest, he sized Little Richard up. Next, (Jesse tells me all this later), Joey walked over to a table, picked up his extra pair of sunglasses and said;

"Put these on and come with me, kid."

Very James Dean.

Joey explained to his young pal that the first thing you need to do is find the right walking stick. He showed Richard the proper technique for choosing a stick and how to use it. Next, he taught him how to throw it down. Jesse heard him saying;

"If you get the right stick it might come right back into your hand."

Is this great material, or what?

Little Richard followed Joey around all day, mimicking his every move. There's much more, but I'll stop here, you get the idea. The important thing is, Richard's confidence swelled. He grew in ways diet and exercise can't affect, and left the mountain with an irreversibly greater measure of self-esteem.

Although we already think the world of him, in our hearts, Joey had grown too.

THE REUNION

Joey returned from paradise declaring that this last week was;

"The best vacation, ever!"

I'm glad it was and hope he feels like saying that, something like that after every adventure he has. Best Vacation, Ever!

During our homecoming hot tub time, I noticed something different about him. A few months ago, he was a round-faced little boy who had decided to get himself in shape this summer. He has. He runs all seven flights of stairs in the building where he lives. He rides his bike and sprints to the corner and back. He runs the skate park like an obstacle course and doesn't drink soda or eat pizza these days. Plus, he's grown a couple of inches. The face looking back at me as we sat in the tub was one of a pre-teen. Still young, but no longer a little boy.

Laura and I chuckled as he told us about Little Richard, a little guy learning how to be a big guy by watching and following Joey's lead. Leader and role-model, our grandson is already demonstrating these qualities.

Another night. The three of us were in the tub again.

Forgetting Quiet Time etiquette, Laura and I had been talking about a couple of kids whose lives had been turned upside-down. Their parents had split-up.

After all this time I should have known. Still, I was surprised that Joey was listening. Hearing me grousing about the behavior of one of these children, he interjected;

"Remember," he corrected me, *"It is not his fault. Collateral damage."*

Typical Joey. I was touched by his empathy.

Incidents like this lead me to say that he's a good guy. Maybe he is, or maybe we're just two more grandparents projecting hope and best wishes on successive generations. Either way, Joey has taught me to be a better human being.

When my boys were young, football season was a big deal. Yes, my boys played, I taught them everything I knew. Fortunately, they had real coaches too. During home games, games played in our yard, I was always the quarterback. Having already decided that there is only one play, time after time I yelled, "Go Long!"

My passes were perfect. If one of the boys missed a catch or fumbled, I would yell at him for being incompetent. As they got older, often as not, I wasn't invited to join the game. More time passed, and I was permanently sidelined. It was a brilliant play designed to put me out of their misery. They had kicked me off the team. Being a parent is equal measures of joy and humiliation. Near as I can tell, the only way you win is by never quitting. Go long.

In many ways, time spent with Joey is not so different. Then again it has been different. I'm different. I raised my sons with genuine concern for their safety and long-term well-being. I faced all that I didn't know, things about how to be someone's Dad. Like every young father, I was trapped between love and terror.

Having Joey with us is the same, but different. The love part, that's the same, maybe even better. Now I'm not held prisoner by all the possibilities, things I knew I couldn't control as a young parent. As a grandfather, I'm free to enjoy the good feelings, the stuff that comes from Joey just being Joey. And me being a lot more relaxed about it all.

Sometimes he humiliates me too, but it feels different. It's funny - most of it's funny. When it's not, I can still laugh. Having seen it all before, there's so much more room in the game. And when he's doing something risky, I think there's a sixth sense or something like it operating, telling me it's going to be okay. Laura suspects that I must have fried too many brain cells, or a bunch of them died of boredom. Either way, the ends of every nerve in my head are not on fire when I see him and his friends throwing the ax around.

The last thing in the world I want is for him to get hurt. Like any other parent or grandparent, I'd sacrifice myself on the front bumper of the Space Shuttle or a speeding 747. But then, both of those are gone! Okay, less dramatic; I would throw myself in front of a truck to save him.

But nowadays, knowing that I won't always be there doesn't wake me up with the sweats in the middle of the night. Not like it did when Kevin was five and the other two were carefully imitating every one of his mistakes.

Now I find an odd comfort in the face of a certainty - the fact that once in a while he's gonna get hurt. I also know that he will learn something important each time it happens.

The humiliation thing? I'd love it if everyone around me, particularly my boys and grandsons thought I was the coolest guy on both sides of the TV screen. When they don't support my fantasies, I'm no longer surprised. I was taught a little humility by my sons, and I'm enjoying the fruits of this bit of maturity in Joey's company. Has anything I've written here been a revelation? Not to parents. Anyone who has raised kids knows that parenting is the fastest method yet invented to make a grown-up grow up.

But there's been this extra thing with Joey, the things he comes up with that are beyond his years, beyond our years. How can I convince readers that Laura and I are not gullible dim-wits? I can't. Maybe that's the purpose of a book like this. You can read stuff Joey said and did and judge for yourself.

So yes, we think Joey's a special kid. At the same time, being realistic for a moment, I suspect that there are others whose abilities would make our favorite genius look average. That's an amazing thing and a whole other story. For now, we're lucky. We've been gifted or something, to be the grandparents of this young boy who's channeling Gandhi and Rodney Dangerfield. Maybe it could be better, but I doubt it. We feel like we won the lottery.

All that to say, Yes, he's inspired me! For example, I'm still thinking about Joey's Cabin in Paradise adventure, still looking for my magic walking stick. So far, no luck. But I'm not giving up. In my spare time I made a Bat Cape, and I plan to run off the shed roof and test my wings.

Yes, I might test these wings real soon. Considering what could happen if something goes wrong when I jump, there's a piece of advice I should pass along now.

This is for Joey and anyone else who might be reading.

Go Long!

ALMOST THE END

Fewer and farther between, but no less entertaining, our adventures with Joey continue to continue. Still, every story must end sometime, and this is probably the right place to flair my Bat Wings and bring this one in for a landing.

Joey will soon be twelve. His life changed dramatically last fall. Recognizing that he needed a wider range of possibilities, his parents enrolled him in public school. It's twenty miles away, but even with the bus ride, he loves everything about it. He loves his all-around larger, twelve-year-old life, particularly the way it's playing on the social scene. He has a wider selection of new friends and attended his first school dance. His parents read it right, he was ready for the big stage. Public School is just the ticket.

All this new activity means that he's here at our house less often. Just the way it works. Of course we still see him. His Mother lives around the corner, so he whips by our house on his skateboard. Often as not, he checks in long enough for Laura to make him a cheeseburger.

Then, like the wind, he's gone.

Even his time in the hot tub is diminishing. If he does want to use it, Joey's polite. He asks us to join him. I suspect he would rather be alone or with his pals. Maybe the sight of a couple of 64-year-old hippies in swimming suits is too much for him. It's okay, we get it!

My three sons and I used to snicker when my grandmother said grace at family dinners. We would wager on how many words she would get out before she started to cry. She was in on the joke. To her credit, she did not care. She loved her family, and that was all that mattered to her.

At the end of grace, her face would be wet with tears, the result of a combination of laughter and other emotions I was not equipped to understand at the time. She'd found the ones she loved, and she kept them close, close to her heart.

Looking back on my record as a parent, I see that I did some things wrong, and I did a few things right. One thing for sure, I know that people are right when they say that it's not about what you give your children, not the stuff. It is about a lot of love and a little guidance. That's it. My grandmother knew these things all along. Your family is all that matters. Her crying was not about sadness. It came from a joy I was not privy to, not equipped to understand - not until I became a grandparent.

Joey recently told us that his spirit animal is a sloth.

This is odd, he's a dinosaur guy. No, this is more than odd. We were surprised by his choice of this particular animal, surprised about the whole notion, the spirit animal thing. It was not an idea we had ever talked about, not our style.

Maybe one of his friends, maybe kids at school adopt spirit animals. Whatever the inspiration, when Joey went looking for one of his own, he returned with this strangest of creatures and a philosophy to go with it.

When asked, he explained it this way;

"Sloths go real slow. And if you go real slow - slow way down, you understand things."

What do you say when your young grandson pops off with that?

Joey didn't choose a frightening, powerful animal. No bears or eagles for this kid. What he says about a sloth, the way he shifted from the sloth to people, delivering a life lesson - maybe someday he'll tell us more. Until then, it's just another example of how our grandson has, and will probably continue to amaze us.

Maybe he will explain, but I think I already know the answer. I think the kid was born knowing how to slow down, knowing how to go slow inside.

Maybe Joey already knows things my grandmother knew. If not, I do not doubt that he will learn real soon.

Our grandson loves his family. Even though his life is accelerating, he stops by, keeping us updated and in his orbit.

Meantime, Joey's finding the new ones, the other ones he will love. I already know that Joey will keep them close.

Made in the USA
Lexington, KY
14 October 2018